The Illustrated
NATHAN BEDFORD FORREST

LOCHLAINN SEABROOK WRITES IN THE FOLLOWING GENRES

Academic
Adventure
Alternate History
American Civil War
American History
American Politics
American South
American West
Anatomy and Physiology
Ancient History
Antiquities
Anthologies
Anthropology
Apocrypha
Aquariology
Archaeology
Art
Art History
Astronomy
Aviation
Aviation History
Behavioral Science
Biblical Exegesis
Biblical Hermeneutics
Bioarchaeology
Biography
Book History
Botany
Camping
Children's Books
Christian Mysticism
Citizen's Rights
Clinical Studies
Coffee Table Books
Coloring Books
Comparative History
Comparative Mythology
Comparative Religion
Conservation
Constitutional Studies
Cooking
Cultural Anthropology
Cultural Geography
Cultural Heritage
Cultural Heritage Studies
Cultural History
Cultural Studies
Cultural Tourism
Cryptozoology
Deep Time Natural History
Destination Guides
Diet and Nutrition
Earth Sciences
Ecology
Ecotourism
Educational
Encyclopediography
Entertainment
Environmental History
Environmental Science
Environmental Studies
Environmental Tourism
Epistemology
Ethnobotany
Ethnology
Ethology
Ethnomusicology
Ethnic Studies
Etymology
European History
Evolutionary Anthropology
Evolutionary Biology
Evolutionary History
Evolutionary Psychology
Exploration
Exobiology

Exposés
Family Histories
Field Guides
Film
Folklore
Forestry
Genealogy
General Audience
Geography
Geology
Genetics
Ghost Stories
Gospels
Guidebooks
Handbooks
Health and Fitness
Heritage Conservation
Heritage Travel
Hiking
Historical Ecology
Historical Fiction
Historical Nonfiction
Historiography
History
History of Ideas
History of Medicine
History of Science
Hobbies and Crafts
Human Evolution
Humanities
Humor
Ichnology
Ichthyology
Illustrated Lost History
Illustrations
Inspirational
Illustrated Zoological Anthologies
Intellectual History
Interdisciplinary Lost Knowledge
Interviews
Journalism
Law of Attraction
Lexicography
Life After Death
Lifestyle
Literary History
Literature
Lost Intellectual Heritage
Lost Knowledge Studies
Lost Treasures
Mammalogy
Marine Biology
Matriarchy
Medical History
Memoir
Men's Studies
Metahistory
Metaphysics
Military
Military History
Museum Studies
Mysteries and Enigmas
Mysticism
Mythology
National Parks
Natural Health
Natural History
Natural Philosophy
Natural Science
Nature
Nature Appreciation
Nature Art
Nonfiction
Oceanography
Onomastics
Outdoor Recreation

Paleoanthropology
Paleoecology
Paleography
Paleoichthyology
Paleontology
Paleozoology
Paranormal
Parapsychology
Parks & Campgrounds
Patriarchy
Patriotism
Performing Arts
Philosophy
Philosophy of Science
Photography
Physical Anthropology
Pictorial
Poetry
Politics
Prehistoric Art
Prehistoric Life
Prehistory
Preservation Studies
Presidential History
Primatology
Primary Documents
Prophecy
Psychology
Quiz
Quotations
Recollections
Reference
Religion
Revolutionary Period
Science
Scripture
Self-help
Social Sciences
Sociology
Southern Culture
Southern Heritage
Southern Narratives
Southern Studies
Southern Traditions
Speeches
Spirituality
Spiritualism
Sport Science
Symbolism
Technology
Thanatology
Thealogy
Theology
Theosophy
Tourism
Travel
UFOlogy
United States
Vanished Works Studies
Vexillology
Victorian Era Studies
Victorian Medicine
Visual Arts
Visual Cultural Memory Studies
Visual Encyclopediography
Visual Natural History
War
Western Civilization
Wildlife
Wildlife Biology
Wildlife Photography
Women's Studies
World History
Writing
Young Adult
Zoology

Mr. Seabrook does not author books for fame and glory, but for the love of writing and sharing his knowledge.

Be curious, not judgmental.

The Illustrated
NATHAN BEDFORD FORREST

An American Patriot's Life in Pictures

LOCHLAINN SEABROOK
BESTSELLING AUTHOR, AWARD-WINNING HISTORIAN, ACCLAIMED ARTIST

Diligently Researched and Generously Illustrated by the Author for the Elucidation of the Reader

2025

Sea Raven Press, Park County, Wyoming USA

THE ILLUSTRATED NATHAN BEDFORD FORREST

Published by
Sea Raven Press, LLC, founded 1995
Park County, Wyoming, USA
SeaRavenPress.com

All text, artwork, and illustrations copyright © Lochlainn Seabrook 2025

in accordance with U.S. and international copyright laws and regulations, as stated and protected under the Berne Union for the Protection of Literary and Artistic Property (Berne Convention), and the Universal Copyright Convention (the UCC). All rights reserved under the Pan-American and International Copyright Conventions.

PRINTING HISTORY
1st SRP paperback edition, 1st printing, October 2025 • ISBN: 978-1-955351-70-6
1st SRP hardcover edition, 1st printing, October 2025 • ISBN: 978-1-955351-71-3

ISBN: 978-1-955351-70-6 (paperback)
Library of Congress Control Number: Registered

This work is the copyrighted intellectual property of Lochlainn Seabrook and has been registered with the Copyright Office at the Library of Congress in Washington, D.C., USA. No part of this work (including text, covers, drawings, photos, illustrations, maps, images, diagrams, etc.), in whole or in part, may be used, reproduced, stored in a retrieval system, or transmitted, in any form or by any means now known or hereafter invented, without written permission from the publisher. The sale, duplication, hire, lending, copying, digitalization, or reproduction of this material, in any manner or form whatsoever, is also prohibited, and is a violation of federal, civil, and digital copyright law, which provides severe civil and criminal penalties for any violations.

The Illustrated Nathan Bedford Forrest: An American Patriot's Life in Pictures, by Lochlainn Seabrook. Includes an introduction and illustrations.

ARTWORK
Front and back cover design and art, book design, layout, font selection, and interior art by Lochlainn Seabrook.
All images, pictures, photos, illustrations, image captions, graphic design, and graphic art copyright © Lochlainn Seabrook.
All images selected, placed, manipulated, cleaned, colored, tinted, and/or created by Lochlainn Seabrook.
Cover image: "At Home with N. B. Forrest," copyright © Lochlainn Seabrook.
All rights reserved.

All persons who approve of the authority and principles of Colonel Lochlainn Seabrook's literary work, and realize its benefits as a means of reeducating the world about facts left out of mainstream books, are hereby requested to avidly recommend his titles to others and to vigorously cooperate in extending their reach, scope, and influence around the globe.

The views documented in this book concerning Forrest, the South, and American history are those of the publisher.

PROUDLY WRITTEN, DESIGNED, AND PUBLISHED IN THE UNITED STATES OF AMERICA.

Dedication

To my cousin Nathan Bedford Forrest, whose indomitable spirit and steadfast faith in God, family, and country will forever inspire all who cherish courage, honor, and truth—and who hold that devotion to principle is the highest measure of man.

Epigraph

"Forrest was the greatest natural genius of the war. He had no military education; yet he was a born soldier—every instinct of war was his by nature."

C.S. General Richard Taylor

1879

CONTENTS

Notes to the Reader ⁕ page 11
Introduction, by Lochlainn Seabrook ⁕ page 13

SECTION 1
EARLY LIFE: ROOTS OF GREATNESS 1821–1849

1. Early Family Portrait ⁕ page 17
2. Birth Home ⁕ page 18
3. Boyhood Home ⁕ page 19
4. Age 12 ⁕ page 20
5. Move to Mississippi ⁕ page 21
6. Hernando Home ⁕ page 22
7. Age 16 ⁕ page 23
8. Horse Trader ⁕ page 24
9. Produce Business ⁕ page 25
10. Texas Independence ⁕ page 26
11. First Land Purchase ⁕ page 27
12. Uncle Jonathan ⁕ page 28
13. Marriage ⁕ page 29
14. The Couple's First Home ⁕ page 30
15. Children ⁕ page 31
16. Looking Westward ⁕ page 32

SECTION 2
MID LIFE: MASTER OF THE FIELD 1850–1869

17. First Memphis Home ⁕ page 35
18. Slave-Trading ⁕ page 36
19. Time Off ⁕ page 37
20. Prosperous Businessman ⁕ page 38
21. Enlistment ⁕ page 39
22. Private Forrest ⁕ page 40
23. First Command ⁕ page 41
24. Officer's Tent ⁕ page 42
25. Battle of Fort Donelson ⁕ page 43
26. Death of Roderick ⁕ page 44
27. Battle of Chickamauga ⁕ page 45
28. Forrest's Black Soldiers ⁕ page 46
29. Battle of Okolona ⁕ page 47
30. Confederate Campfire ⁕ page 48
31. Battle of Brice's Cross Roads ⁕ page 49
32. Battle of Johnsonville ⁕ page 50
33. Battle of Franklin ⁕ page 51
34. Surrender at Gainesville ⁕ page 52
35. Homecoming ⁕ page 53
36. Postwar Rebuilding ⁕ page 54

SECTION 3
FINAL YEARS: LEGACY & REDEMPTION 1870–1877

37. Green Grove Plantation ❧ page 57
38. New Memphis Home ❧ page 58
39. Democratic National Convention Delegate ❧ page 59
40. Railwayman ❧ page 60
41. Confederate Veterans Reunion ❧ page 61
42. Final Home on President's Island ❧ page 62
43. The Pole Bearers' Address ❧ page 63
44. Conversion ❧ page 64
45. Forrest Takes Ill ❧ page 65
46. Passing of an American Icon ❧ page 66
47. Funeral Procession ❧ page 67
48. Elmwood Cemetery ❧ page 68
49. Reinterment and Monument Unveiling ❧ page 69
50. Forrest Remembered ❧ page 70

Meet the Author-Historian-Artist ❧ page 71
Praise for the Author ❧ page 73
Learn More ❧ page 75

July 1863, northern Alabama. General Forrest strategizes "in the saddle," carefully calculating his next move. Known for his restless energy and constant mobility, the legendary commander often issued his military dispatches while "on the road." Copyright © Lochlainn Seabrook.

NOTES TO THE READER

THE ARTISTIC CREATIVE PROCESS
☛ Due to the nature of creating an art-based coffee table book, please note that my images are not necessarily drawn to scale, or in many cases, not even according to actual reality. In consequence, my illustrations may contain historical inaccuracies concerning such items as military rank, architectural dimensions, the number of stars on flags, colors and styles of uniforms, etc.

NEW WORD
☛ On page 36 I use a word that I coined specifically for this book, *presentist*: Someone who unfairly judges the past through the narrow lens of contemporary mores, social norms, customs, conventions, values, traditions, and ideologies. Presentism, a common strategy used by enemies of the Truth to obscure the facts and rewrite authentic history, has been one of the primary weapons employed against Forrest. This book will aid in undoing some of the damage done to his name and memory by modern day presentists.

FURTHER EDUCATION
☛ Interested in learning more about the man British Commander-in-Chief Garnet Wolseley called "nature's soldier"? Pick up a copy of my book, *A Rebel Born: A Defense of Nathan Bedford Forrest*, for which I was awarded the UDC's prestigious Jefferson Davis Historical Gold Medal, and which *Confederate Veteran* magazine calls "the definitive Forrest biography." For a complete list of my literary works, visit SeaRavenPress.com or LochlainnSeabrook.com. L.S.

"Southern hero, American patriot."

While Forrest's cavalry horses rest between battles, a loyal camp dog keeps watch. Copyright © Lochlainn Seabrook.

INTRODUCTION

Forrest in 1850, age 29.

WHEN THE NAME NATHAN BEDFORD FORREST is mentioned, most people think only of "that famous Confederate general" or "that superlative cavalryman." Yet it must be remembered that his time in the C.S. army lasted barely four years—though it surely felt much longer to him.

My book, *The Illustrated Nathan Bedford Forrest*, examines not only those four years, in which he emerged as one of the world's greatest military leaders and tacticians, but also the other fifty-two years of his comparatively brief life: the period in which he grew from an energetic country boy into a seasoned mountain man; from a roughhewn frontiersman into a gentle husband and devoted father; and from a lower middle-class laborer into a genteel Tennessee multimillionaire, successful Southern businessman, and deservedly lionized American entrepreneur.

In addition to this broader focus on Forrest's civilian life—both antebellum and postbellum—another major goal of this work is to provide new artistic impressions of his life as a whole. To accomplish this, I have divided his biography into three sections: early life, mid life, and final years. This structure allows me to visually explore nearly every phase and dimension of his 56 years—personal, business, military, and social—many of which have never before been artistically recreated. In fact, this volume is the first, and at present the only, work of its kind.

While most of my images are necessarily hypothetical, each one is firmly grounded in historical data—drawn from my other twelve books on Forrest. Inevitably, when dealing with a man born more than two centuries ago, some details remain uncertain or disputed. Forrest's life, like a great puzzle, includes missing pieces and contradictions, often arising from the biases, faulty memories, or errors of early biographers. For that reason, I have deliberately avoided the so-called "mainstream" accounts of his life, which amount to little more than a mixture of vitriolic misinformation, disinformation, and malinformation—utterly useless to honest historians and ethical scholars seeking to preserve authentic history.

The Illustrated Nathan Bedford Forrest will not only appeal to longtime admirers of the General, but it will also inspire new respect and understanding among those unfamiliar with his true character. It is designed to reintroduce this exemplary gentleman to a modern audience and to help restore the truth about his extraordinary life—truth long obscured by a century and a half of malicious distortion, baseless defamation, and politically motivated falsehoods.

It is time to clear Forrest's name and to restore his rightful place among America's great conservatives, patriots, and racial unifiers. May this book aid in that goal.

Lochlainn Seabrook
Park County, Wyoming, USA
October 2025

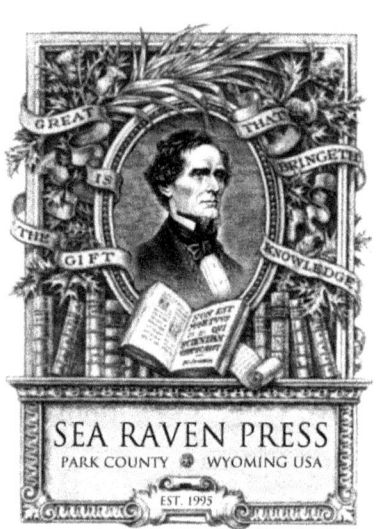

"Books invite all; they constrain none."
Hartley Burr Alexander (1873-1939)

SECTION I

Early Life: Roots of Greatness

1821-1849

EARLY FAMILY PORTRAIT

1821, near Chapel Hill, Tennessee. My hypothetical artistic reconstruction of Forrest's parents: William Forrest (age 27), a blacksmith, and Mariam Beck (age 24), a homemaker—holding their firstborn child, Nathan Bedford Forrest, who entered this world on July 13, 1821. William was of English and possibly Scottish stock, Mariam was of Irish, Scottish, and possibly Scandinavian stock. All illustrations copyright © Lochlainn Seabrook.

BIRTH HOME

Circa mid 1820s, near Chapel Hill, Tennessee. A hypothetical artistic reconstruction of Forrest's birthplace (a one-room cabin with loft). The family lived here until about 1830. The structure has long since disappeared, with only a lone historical plaque to indicate its former approximate location. Copyright © Lochlainn Seabrook.

BOYHOOD HOME

1830, near Chapel Hill, Tennessee. Nine year old Nathan skillfully guides a rolling hoop with his trundle stick in the popular Victorian children's game of Hoop and Stick. He and his friends are playing in front of what is today known as "Nathan Bedford Forrest's Boyhood Home." William moved his family here in 1830, where they lived until about 1833 or so. Thus the young Tennessean spent some of his most important developmental years in this house, from ages 9 to 12. The home still stands, and has been visited and photographed numerous times by the author-artist. Copyright © Lochlainn Seabrook.

AGE 12

1833, near Chapel Hill, Tennessee. Young Nathan enjoyed nature, working with livestock, and helping out on his parents' homestead. His formative years as a farmboy ingrained in him a lifelong love for agriculture, animals (particularly horses), and the out-of-doors. Copyright © Lochlainn Seabrook.

MOVE TO MISSISSIPPI

1833-1834. Top row: William (age 37) and Mariam (age 34) moving their young family to the now extinct town of Salem, Mississippi, around 1834, in hopes of a brighter future. (The village would later be destroyed by Union troops during Lincoln's War.) Middle left: Nathan (age 13), lower right: Frances (age 10), lower left: John (age 8). Copyright © Lochlainn Seabrook.

HERNANDO HOME

The Forrest family's modest home in Hernando, Mississippi, circa 1836-1843. After William's death in 1837, Nathan, now 16, became the head of the household, catapulting him suddenly from the somewhat carefree world of adolescence into adulthood with all its serious responsibilities. Copyright © Lochlainn Seabrook.

AGE 16

As the eldest son, Forrest was burdened with numerous responsibilities, among them protection of the family. However, his inherent love of the outdoors, firearms, hunting, and horses meant that he excelled at this particular obligation, as the following story from 1837 demonstrates. One day his mother Mariam, carrying a basket of baby chickens, and her sister Fanny Beck were returning on horseback from a visit with a neighbor. Lured by the sight, sounds, and smell of the poultry, a mountain lion suddenly sprung from a bush sinking its claws into Mariam and her horse. The two terrified ladies managed to scare off the huge cat and gallop home. Upon hearing the story, 16 year old Nathan promised to avenge his family. Leaping onto his horse, he tore off out of the yard with his three dogs, Nero, Plunger, and Gammon, following closely behind. It was not long before the excitable lad located the puma perched high in a tree. As it spat and hissed at his dogs, he took careful aim, bringing down the angry feline with a single shot through the heart. It was true stories like this that became the foundation for what was to become the "legend of Nathan Bedford Forrest." Copyright © Lochlainn Seabrook.

HORSE TRADER

After his father's death in 1837, the always enterprising young Nathan took on several new ventures to help support his mother and siblings. Among these was horse trading—a pursuit in which his sharp eye for fine horseflesh quickly set him apart. By 1838, at just 17 years old, he had already earned a countywide reputation for restoring undervalued and neglected horses to health and selling them at a profit. Copyright © Lochlainn Seabrook.

PRODUCE BUSINESS

Other businesses he started included cattle trading, farming, land speculation, and small-scale mercantile trade. Here, in 1839, the 18 year old is trying his hand at selling produce, a successful business aided by two of his brothers, John (age 15), back left, and Aaron (age 13), lower left. Copyright © Lochlainn Seabrook.

TEXAS INDEPENDENCE

Always a diehard American conservative and patriot, in February 1841, 19 year old Nathan became a volunteer in the Mississippi militia at Holly Springs, hoping to aid in Texas' fight for independence. By the time he and his fellow soldiers arrived in Houston, however, the conflict had subsided, and he was forced to split rails on a local plantation to earn enough money to return to his mother's house. The brief military foray was not a complete loss. During his time on the Texas farm, Nathan learned how to run and operate a large-scale agricultural holding, an idea that excited him, and one that would soon help turn him into one of the wealthiest men in America. Copyright © Lochlainn Seabrook.

FIRST LAND PURCHASE

In late 1841, the now 20 year old Nathan seems to have made his first land purchase. Using savings from his early business ventures in horse and cattle trading, he bought a small tract of land in Marshall County, Mississippi, near Salem (not far from the Tennessee border). This small-scale land acquisition marked the beginning of his career as a landowner and future business mogul, a foundation that would later expand into large-scale antebellum operations in real estate, cotton trading, and eventually the slave trade. Copyright © Lochlainn Seabrook.

UNCLE JONATHAN

Noting his nephew's successes with horses, cattle, and real estate, in the fall of 1842 Nathan's Uncle Jonathan Forrest (right) invited the 21 year old to become a junior business partner in his mercantile and horse-trading enterprise at Hernando, Mississippi. Nathan jumped at the chance to move out of his widowed mother's house to begin carving out his own destiny. (A year later, in 1843, Mariam would marry Joseph Luxton—with whom she eventually had four more children, Nathan's half-siblings.) Tragically, in 1845, only three years later, Jonathan was gunned down during a dispute with several local troublemakers. Nathan avenged his uncle's death by ridding Hernando of the ne'er-do-wells, and for his heroism appreciative town authorities promptly elected him constable of Hernando and coroner of DeSoto County. Copyright © Lochlainn Seabrook.

MARRIAGE

On September 25, 1845, despite mild protest by her influential uncle, Reverend Samuel Montgomery Cowan, 24 year old Nathan married sophisticated high-society girl Mary Ann Montgomery at Hernando, Mississippi. An 1845 illustration of the newlyweds reveals that Forrest shaved off his famous beard for the occasion. Unfortunately, the romantic idyll between the rough-and-tumble frontiersman and the pretty 19 year old Southern belle would be interrupted in 1861 by Lincoln's unconstitutional (and therefore illegal) invasion of the Southern states. Despite this, the couple's devoted love marked the beginning of a lifelong union, one rooted in deep affection and mutual respect, and which endured through all of Forrest's later military and business successes, hardships, and final years. Copyright © Lochlainn Seabrook.

THE COUPLE'S FIRST HOME

My hypothetical artistic reconstruction of Nathan and Mary Ann's first home together, at Hernando, Mississippi. They lived in this modest yet dignified mid 19th-Century dwelling from 1845 to 1851, bearing two children during their six year stay. Architecturally, the home—which perfectly suited the young, upwardly mobile couple—represented the transitional style between frontier simplicity and early Southern prosperity: functional, well-built, and indicative of a family beginning to rise in financial means and social standing. Copyright © Lochlainn Seabrook.

CHILDREN

Nathan and Mary Ann's two children: 8 year old William "Willie" Montgomery Forrest (1846-1908), and 5 year old Frances "Fanny" Forrest (1849-1854), both born in Hernando, Mississippi. Sadly, Frances passed away from dysentery in early 1854, a crushing blow for her loving, doting parents. Willie, however, would go on to become his famous father's aid-de-camp, and later a captain on his staff, during Lincoln's War. Copyright © Lochlainn Seabrook.

LOOKING WESTWARD

A young Nathan Bedford Forrest glances westward, symbolizing his courage, strength, vision, and hope for a better future for all of America. This fierce, forward-looking spirit would fortify him for what was soon to come: Not only fabulous fame and fortune, but an illicit, unjust, and unnecessary war between the liberal North and the conservative South—still one of most misunderstood and most intentionally misrepresented conflicts in world history. Copyright © Lochlainn Seabrook.

SECTION 2

Mid Life: Master of the Field

1850-1869

FIRST MEMPHIS HOME

In his steady rise toward success, in 1851 Nathan moved his young family to the thriving river port of Memphis, Tennessee. There he and Mary Ann established their first Memphis residence on the city's famed "Millionaire's Row." Situated at approximately 190 Adams Avenue (near present-day North 3rd Street), the grand antebellum mansion—built around 1851—stood as a proud symbol of Forrest's pre-war prosperity and ambition. The impressive house vanished long ago, a victim of the upheavals of Lincoln's War, the collapse of the Southern economy, and the relentless march of urban expansion. Copyright © Lochlainn Seabrook.

SLAVE-TRADING

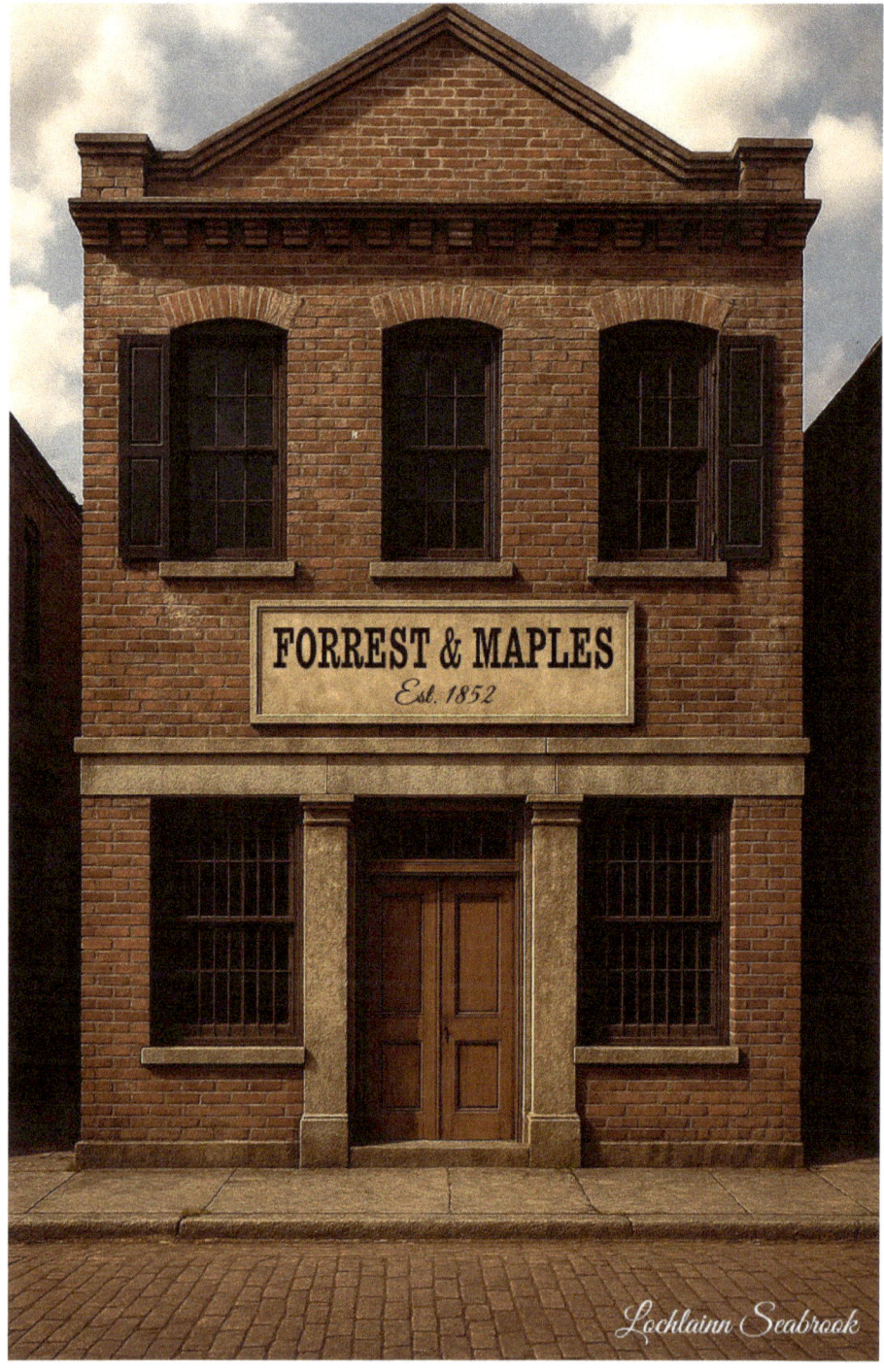

1852, Forrest's slave-trading office at 87 Adams St., Memphis. Today's presentists (those who unfairly judge the past through the narrow lens of contemporary social norms) often criticize Forrest for his work as a slave-trader, attributing to him all of the ugly stereotypes that usually go along with that profession. However, the facts do not support these charges. First, he was only in the business for five years (1852-1857), selling the enterprise and freeing all of his own personal servants in 1857—six full years before Lincoln issued his fake Emancipation Proclamation (which was not actually intended to abolish slavery). Second, in 1852 slavery was legal in all 32 states in the Union—including *all* of the Northern states. Third, Forrest was known far and wide as a fair, kind, and humanitarian slaver who kept the blacks under his care clean, well-clothed, and well-fed, even encouraging them to learn to read and write. He also refused to separate slave families, taking a financial loss to purchase entire families rather than splitting them up. On several occasions he even spent his own time and money to go in search of lost black kin that had been separated during earlier sales, buying the whole clan in order to reunite them with their loved ones. Fourth, eyewitnesses report that African Americans, aware of Forrest's reputation as a benevolent and lenient businessman, lined up outside his office begging to be purchased by him. Copyright © Lochlainn Seabrook.

TIME OFF

1858: In a rare moment of peace and quiet, Nathan and Mary Ann enjoy each other's company in their Memphis parlor. Copyright © Lochlainn Seabrook.

PROSPEROUS BUSINESSMAN

Checking the ledgers. Thanks to his industrious work ethic, focused energies, superior intelligence, and entrepreneurial spirit, by 1860, one year before the start of Lincoln's War, Forrest was worth an estimated $1.5 million—about $550 million in today's currency. As I note in my book *A Rebel Born*, considering that he owned thousands of acres of real estate and numerous homes and plantations, and dabbled in dozens of other businesses as well, this figure is no doubt quite conservative. Copyright © Lochlainn Seabrook.

ENLISTMENT

According to Forrest, during the November 1860 presidential race he had cast his vote "for peace." That having failed with the election of the warmongering Liberal Abraham Lincoln (who quickly began appointing socialists and communists to his administration and armies), on June 14, 1861, Forrest marched—along with his youngest brother Jeffrey and his son Willie (far right)—down to the local recruiting office in Memphis and enlisted as a private in the Confederate army. Thus began what would become one of the most remarkable careers in the annals of military history. Copyright © Lochlainn Seabrook.

PRIVATE FORREST

Private Forrest—a lifelong conservative and ardent constitutionalist who deeply resented Liberal Lincoln's intrusion into Southern affairs—as he appeared during his first month as a C.S. soldier. Though he entered the army at the lowest rank, his time as a private was brief. His natural leadership, fearlessness, extraordinary equestrianism, crack marksmanship, and imposing physical presence quickly set him apart from lesser men, earning him a reputation as one of the most formidable warriors in the Confederate military—one whom thousands of Confederate soldiers would come to love and follow, and one whom thousands of Union soldiers would come to dread facing on the battlefield. Copyright © Lochlainn Seabrook.

FIRST COMMAND

Instantly garnering attention as a born leader who was virtually worshiped by his men, C.S. officials were quick to advance Forrest in rank. Thus, after raising and personally equipping his own cavalry, he was promoted from private to lieutenant colonel on October 30, 1861. The unit, known as Forrest's Cavalry Battalion, later became part of the famed Tennessee Mounted Rifles. Here Lt. Col. Forrest leads his new "critter company" under the Confederacy's 11 star First National Flag. The C.S.A. never repaid Forrest for his personal financial investments (which numbered in the millions of dollars), as Lincoln's War shut down the C.S. government and bankrupted the South. Copyright © Lochlainn Seabrook.

OFFICER'S TENT

December 1861, Forrest in his field tent, Hopkinsville, Kentucky. Newly appointed as a lieutenant colonel, Forrest confers with his aide-de-camp (back left) while reviewing campaign maps. One of his trusted bodyguards keeps a watchful eye. The young officer's natural tactical genius and daring exploits on the field of action would soon earn him worldwide acclaim. Copyright © Lochlainn Seabrook.

BATTLE OF FORT DONELSON

February 11-16, 1862: Battle of Fort Donelson. The Confederate stronghold at Fort Donelson on the Cumberland River came under massive assault by Yankee troops led by Union General Ulysses S. Grant. Trapped in the freezing cold with little hope of victory, most Southern officers agreed to surrender. One cavalry leader, however, refused to capitulate. Rallying his men, Forrest organized a bold breakout through encircling Union lines and escaped with his command intact into the snowy back country. This audacious act of defiance became the first of many legendary exploits that would define Forrest's remarkable military career. Copyright © Lochlainn Seabrook.

DEATH OF RODERICK

March 5, 1863, Battle of Thompson's Station. During the fight, Brigadier General Forrest's favorite warhorse, Roderick, was struck three times by enemy fire then sent to the rear for treatment. Moments later, hearing his master's voice leading another charge, the devoted steed broke free from his handlers. Leaping three fences to reach him, Roderick was shot a fourth time—this time fatally. The heartbroken Confederate officer buried his faithful companion where he fell, a grave that can still be seen to this day. Copyright © Lochlainn Seabrook.

BATTLE OF CHICKAMAUGA

September 18, 1863, Battle of Chickamauga. Clad in his trademark white linen duster and bristling with weapons, a wild-eyed Forrest stands alone atop a mist-shrouded hill in the gray Georgia dawn yearning for the fight to begin. Sighting the enemy below, he raises his revolver and fires the first shot of the conflict—a single thunderclap that shatters the morning calm, unleashing one of the bloodiest clashes of the war. Copyright © Lochlainn Seabrook.

FORREST'S BLACK SOLDIERS

Riding at the head of his cavalry, General Forrest chats amiably with one of the 65 black men he enlisted to fight alongside him during the war—seven of whom he assigned to serve as his personal armed bodyguards. Friendship, mutual respect, and racial integration (which, unlike Union troops, were racially segregated) was the norm in Forrest's command, with all African American soldiers being promised unconditional emancipation for their service. After the war, when asked about these particular soldiers, Forrest proudly replied: "These boys stayed with me, drove my teams, and better Confederates did not live." Decades later, Forrest's surviving black soldiers continued to attend Confederate veterans reunions, where they were warmly welcomed by their white comrades. Copyright © Lochlainn Seabrook.

BATTLE OF OKOLONA

February 22, 1864, Battle of Okolona. Here Brigadier General Forrest commands his cavalry in a fierce engagement against Yankee forces under U.S. General William Sooy Smith. Despite being outnumbered, Forrest's skillful tactics and relentless pursuit forced a decisive Union retreat. Another Confederate triumph. Copyright © Lochlainn Seabrook.

CONFEDERATE CAMPFIRE

May 1864: Major General Forrest relaxes with his men around a campfire in northern Mississippi, just weeks before his stunning victory at Brice's Cross Roads. Copyright © Lochlainn Seabrook.

BATTLE OF BRICE'S CROSS ROADS

June 10, 1864, The Battle of Brice's Cross Roads. Against overwhelming odds, Major General Forrest leads his vastly outnumbered cavalry to one of the most brilliant victories of the war. Through sheer audacity, tactical genius, and unshakeable discipline, he turned chaos into triumph—routing a superior Union force and cementing his reputation as one of history's greatest natural military commanders. Copyright © Lochlainn Seabrook.

BATTLE OF JOHNSONVILLE

November 4-5, 1864, Battle of Johnsonville. Major General Forrest directs his artillery and cavalry from the bluffs overlooking the Tennessee River as Union supply depots and gunboats erupt in flames below. Forrest's daring surprise raid on Johnsonville resulted in the destruction of millions of dollars' worth of Federal supplies, crippling Union river operations in western Tennessee and humiliating Yankee officials. Copyright © Lochlainn Seabrook.

BATTLE OF FRANKLIN

November 30, 1864, Battle of Franklin (II). Major General Forrest commands his cavalry with his usual courage and precision as the great Confederate assault unfolds near Carnton Plantation, just south of Nashville. Though not in overall command, Forrest's seasoned troopers fought valiantly, covering the flanks and later protecting the retreat in one of the War's bloodiest encounters. The desperate struggle under the cold Tennessee moon left thousands of gallant Southern soldiers dead or wounded. Yet Forrest once again proved his mastery of leadership and his unbroken resolve in the face of overwhelming odds. Copyright © Lochlainn Seabrook.

SURRENDER AT GAINESVILLE

May 9, 1865, Gainesville, Alabama. Lieutenant General Forrest, calm and resolute, formally surrenders his cavalry command to Union forces under Yankee Major General Edward Hatch. With the Confederacy collapsing around him, Forrest closes his legendary military career with dignity and honor, reminding his men to "obey the laws, preserve their honor, and become good citizens." Forrest was the only man on either side of the War—South or North—to rise from private to lieutenant general (one rank shy of full general), a distinction that underscores the patriotic Tennessean's unparalleled natural military genius, valor, and patriotism. Unusual for "Civil War" generals, between 1861 and 1865 some 20,000 men served under him in one capacity or another, a reflection of both his personal magnetism and his exceptional ability to recruit, lead, and inspire his soldiers. He was the only major Confederate general without formal military schooling; and in fact he had only a limited formal education as a boy. Everything Forrest knew about warfare came from experience, observation, and instinct. In other words, he mastered strategy, tactics, logistics, and leadership through intuition, ingenuity, and sheer will, qualities that ensure his battlefield principles will continue to be studied at military academies around the world. Copyright © Lochlainn Seabrook.

HOMECOMING

Circa May 21, 1865: After four long years of unrelenting combat, a war-weary General Forrest—heartbroken over Lee's surrender and fully prepared to continue the fight—returns home to his beloved Memphis. Though his battered uniform bears evidence of countless difficult campaigns, his spirit remains unbroken. The townspeople—white and black alike—turn out in celebration to welcome home the man who has become a living legend and who risked his life to "save the South." With characteristic modesty and quiet strength, Forrest greets the crowd with an attitude that speaks of endurance, faith, and reconciliation. Copyright © Lochlainn Seabrook.

POSTWAR REBUILDING

Circa 1866. Having lost nearly everything during Lincoln's War, General Forrest returns to Memphis determined to rebuild both his fortunes and his community. Here, he stands before his war-ravaged home, supervising its restoration—a symbol of his own perseverance and the South's enduring spirit. Copyright © Lochlainn Seabrook.

SECTION 3

Final Years: Legacy & Redemption

1870-1877

GREEN GROVE PLANTATION

Circa 1866, Green Grove Plantation, Sunflower Landing, Mississippi. In the difficult years following Lincoln's War, Forrest and his adoring wife Mary Ann returned to their sprawling 3,000-acre estate, "Green Grove," on the Mississippi River. Here, amid the rich delta soil and the slow rhythm of river life, the now world famous military leader began rebuilding his shattered fortune through farming and trade, hiring freedmen and freedwomen, many of them his former servants, to assist him. This scene captures a brief but hopeful chapter in the life of a proud and industrious Southern gentleman determined to rise again. Copyright © Lochlainn Seabrook.

NEW MEMPHIS HOME

After selling Green Grove Plantation in 1867, Forrest and Mary Ann returned to Memphis, where, using profits from his two years at Green Grove, he built a handsome new home, launching the next chapter of their lives. Though his massive wealth was gone, his resolve remained intact. In this new residence—modest by antebellum standards yet dignified and comfortable—Forrest worked tirelessly to rebuild his fortunes and reputation amid the turbulent years of Reconstruction. Here, the couple stand together as symbols of strength, faith, and Southern perseverance in the face of profound change. Copyright © Lochlainn Seabrook.

DEMOCRATIC NATIONAL CONVENTION DELEGATE

July 4, 1868, New York City. In the summer of 1868 Forrest—like a majority of other Southerners then as now, a dyed-in-the-wool political Conservative—was one of 49 distinguished Southerners chosen to serve as delegates at the first postwar Democratic National Convention. (Note that at this time the Democrats were America's Conservative Party, while the Republicans were the Liberal Party—an arrangement that would not change until the election of 1896, when the two sides switched platforms becoming the parties we know today.) By now an international celebrity, the General's appearance at the assembly drew worldwide attention, causing a sensation among attendees. At first he supported Andrew Johnson—until it was decided that the "Tennessee Tailor" could not win. Forrest then quickly switched, casting his vote for Conservative Democrat and New York Governor Horatio Seymour. Unfortunately for the still prostrate South, the presidential win went to Union General Ulysses S. Grant, an outcome the right-wing Tennessean could not have been happy about: Not only was Grant a Republican—then a Liberal, but he was also one of the men who tried to hunt down and murder Forrest during Lincoln's War. Copyright © Lochlainn Seabrook.

RAILWAYMAN

Circa 1868-1871. Partly in an effort to increase his income, around this time Forrest embarked on a longtime dream with his son Willie: The construction of a railway line that would connect Memphis, Tennessee, with Selma, Alabama, a patriotic postwar effort meant to help rebuild the shattered South, whose infrastructure had been nearly completely destroyed by Lincoln and his illegal assault on the C.S.A., the Southern people, and the U.S. Constitution. Of his railway venture Forrest remarked: "I want our country quiet once more, and I want to see our people united and working together harmoniously." Forrest took on the role of company president, forming "N. B. Forrest and Son," which oversaw grading, construction, and engineering work. As part of this bold reconstruction plan, the General sought out the best workers he knew, hiring some 400 blacks to help with the massive project—not just as laborers, but also as architects, engineers, conductors, foremen, and skilled tradesmen. (As further refutation of Forrest's so-called "racism," after his black employees' one-year contract ran out, all but fifteen of the men returned to continue working for him.) Ultimately, the railway failed, a victim of equipment shortages, dishonest financiers, a yellow fever outbreak, and the Panic of 1873. The collapse of the Selma, Marion, and Memphis Railroad, into which Forrest had invested most of his remaining savings, meant further financial problems for the aging former multimillionaire. Filing for bankruptcy cleared his debts, but did not resolve mounting financial pressures. Copyright © Lochlainn Seabrook.

CONFEDERATE VETERANS REUNION

In the early 1870s Forrest began attending informal Confederate veterans reunions, an enjoyable way for the aging war hero to celebrate old friendships and the shared memories of military service. Naturally, he was often asked to speak before his former soldiers, speeches in which he emphasized American unity, reconciliation between North and South, and racial unity across Dixie. Copyright © Lochlainn Seabrook.

FINAL HOME ON PRESIDENT'S ISLAND

Around 1874, using his last remaining capital, Forrest leased a double log cabin on a twelve-mile long, 32,000 acre piece of land called President's Island, located in the Mississippi River just south of Memphis. The largest island on the "Big Muddy," he hired some 100 white and black men and women to work the 1,300 acre property. With his health now declining, it would be the last private residence the General would ever live in. Copyright © Lochlainn Seabrook.

THE POLE BEARERS' ADDRESS

July 4, 1875, Memphis, Tennessee. On Independence Day 1875 Forrest speaks, by invitation, before a public gathering of the Independent Order of Pole Bearers—a black-only fraternal organization and a forerunner of today's NAACP. The General was warmly welcomed by the group, and was even presented with a beautiful bouquet of flowers, making the tough old Confederate chieftain blush with pride. Visibly moved, he responded to the crowd with his usual affection and gratitude, speaking of, not bitterness or division, but of reconciliation, friendship, and shared hope for the future. Forrest spoke sincerely of peace and goodwill between the races and pledged his support to any African American who might seek his aid. His words, and the grace with which they were received, symbolized a noble gesture toward unity during a time when our country was still struggling to heal its wounds. Copyright © Lochlainn Seabrook.

CONVERSION

Autumn 1875. Forrest's increasingly failing health no doubt caused him to reflect more seriously on the future state of his soul. This, along with years of Mary Ann's earnest prayers for her husband's salvation, finally prompted the graying war chief to fully convert to Christianity. On November 14, 1875, Forrest was baptized at the Cumberland Presbyterian Church of Memphis, turning his life over to Jesus, whom he began referring to as "my Lord and Savior." Forrest's spiritual rebirth had a profound impact on him. Among other things, he dropped all of his lawsuits—even though his attorneys assured him that they were winnable and that they would have enabled him to recoup most of his financial losses. In response to these matters he replied: "I am broken in spirit and have not long to live. My life has been a battle from the start.... I have seen too much violence, and I want to close my days in peace with all the world, as I am now at peace with my Maker." Copyright © Lochlainn Seabrook.

FORREST TAKES ILL

By the summer of 1877 Forrest's health began to decline even more rapidly. Knowing the end was near, he gave his last public appearance on September 21, 1877, at a reunion of the Seventh Tennessee Regiment of Cavalry in Memphis—the same regiment he had enlisted in as a private sixteen years earlier. The malarial swamps of President's Island was no place for the ailing celebrity, so in late October of that year, friends and family had him taken to his brother Jesse's home in Memphis. Old friends visited him, including President Jefferson Davis. At 7:15 pm on October 29th, now down to a mere 100 lbs. in weight, Forrest silently passed away from exhaustion, high blood pressure related issues, malaria, chronic dysentery, diabetic complications, and the effects of a spinal wound he had received at the Battle of Shiloh. At 56 years of age he was still young, even by Victorian standards. His death was widely reported, his obituary noting that Forrest had met his end with religious composure and complete acceptance. Copyright © Lochlainn Seabrook.

PASSING OF AN AMERICAN ICON

October 31, 1877, Memphis, Tennessee. General Forrest lies in peaceful repose as mourners gather to bid farewell to the South's great cavalry leader. Copyright © Lochlainn Seabrook.

FUNERAL PROCESSION

October 31, 1877, Memphis, Tennessee. Forrest's funeral procession through town stretched for 3 miles, from his brother Jesse's home all the way to Elmwood Cemetery. The General's casket was carried in a black hearse pulled by black horses. President Jefferson Davis was in attendance, as were soldiers from his command, various Confederate veterans groups, horsemen, firemen, policemen, everyday citizens, black workers from his President's Island plantation, and a brass band playing the *Dead March*. The local papers made special notice of the fact that "thousands of grieving African Americans" also showed up to pay their respects to Forrest, hundreds of them marching solemnly in his funeral procession. Copyright © Lochlainn Seabrook.

ELMWOOD CEMETERY

1877, Memphis, Tennessee. My hypothetical image of Forrest's original grave at Elmwood Cemetery in Memphis. Following his death on October 29, 1877, Forrest was laid to rest in Memphis' Elmwood Cemetery beside his devoted wife, Mary Ann Montgomery Forrest. His modest marble headstone probably bore his military title and "Confederate States Army," while Mary Ann's marked her as the "Wife of Lt. Gen. N. B. Forrest." In keeping with Southern custom, Confederate flags and floral tributes were no doubt regularly placed at the General's grave by citizens and veterans who regarded him as one of America's greatest military and social leaders, the literal "Spiritual Comforter of the Southern People," as he was widely known. This quiet setting beneath the cemetery's ancient oak trees became known as a hallowed place of reflection and homage—until 1904. Copyright © Lochlainn Seabrook.

REINTERMENT & MONUMENT UNVEILING

On November 11, 1904, the remains of Confederate General Nathan Bedford Forrest and his wife, Mary Ann Montgomery Forrest, were reinterred with great ceremony at downtown Forrest Park in Memphis, Tennessee. Their transfer from Elmwood Cemetery was organized by Confederate veterans and civic leaders to honor Forrest's military genius and to provide a central memorial site for the public. At the same event a massive bronze equestrian statue of Forrest—sculpted by Charles Henry Niehaus—was unveiled atop a marble pedestal, becoming one of Memphis' most prominent landmarks for over a century. In December 2017, however, under cover of night, the statue and remains were illegally removed by the City of Memphis in violation of state heritage protection laws. The city had sold the park to a private entity to circumvent the Tennessee Heritage Protection Act, which forbids removal of historical monuments from public property. After a lengthy legal and restoration process, the remains of General and Mrs. Forrest were respectfully reinterred on September 18, 2021, at Historic Elm Springs, in Columbia, Tennessee, national headquarters of the Sons of Confederate Veterans. The couple may now at last rest in peace. Copyright © Lochlainn Seabrook.

FORREST REMEMBERED

My final image captures the indomitable spirit of General Nathan Bedford Forrest—a man whose brilliance, courage, and unshakable determination made him what I and many others believe was one of America's greatest military men. From humble beginnings on the Tennessee frontier to national prominence as a self-made multimillionaire, fearless warrior, and later a voice for racial unity and sectional reconciliation, Forrest's life embodied discipline, honor, and devotion to duty. His legendary tactical genius earned him respect even from his former foes, while his later years revealed a man transformed by faith, striving to heal a divided republic. In a futile attempt to rewrite history, his sacred resting place at Memphis' Forrest Park was violated by the historically ignorant, the socially vindictive, and the politically malevolent. Yet like the constitutional principles he fought for, his memory cannot be destroyed. In the hearts of countless admirers, he remains a symbol of Southern valor, self-reliance, and perseverance—a true patriot whose legacy continues to inspire those who honor truth, heritage, courage, and above all Americanism. Indeed, if he had lived into his 60s, I believe that the Democrat Party—then America's Conservative Party—would have nominated Forrest for U.S. president. Copyright © Lochlainn Seabrook.

MEET THE AUTHOR-ARTIST

"Bestselling author, award-winning historian, and esteemed nature writer and artist Lochlainn Seabrook straddles multiple genres with ease, seamlessly weaving together history, science, politics, philosophy, and spirituality with the authority of a scholar and the flair of a storyteller." — SEA RAVEN PRESS

AMERICAN POLYMATH LOCHLAINN SEABROOK is a bestselling author, award-winning historian, and acclaimed multidisciplinary artist. A descendant of the families of Alexander Hamilton Stephens, John Singleton Mosby, Edmund Winchester Rucker, and William Giles Harding, the neo-Victorian scholar is a 7th generation Kentuckian, and one of the most prolific and widely read traditional writers in the world today. Known by literary critics as the "new Shelby Foote," the "American Robert Graves," the "Southern Joseph Campbell," and the "Rocky Mountain Richard Jefferies," and by his fans as the "the best author ever," he is a recipient of the United Daughters of the Confederacy's prestigious Jefferson Davis Historical Gold Medal, and is considered the foremost Southern interpreter of American Civil War history—or what he refers to as the War for the Constitution (1861-1865).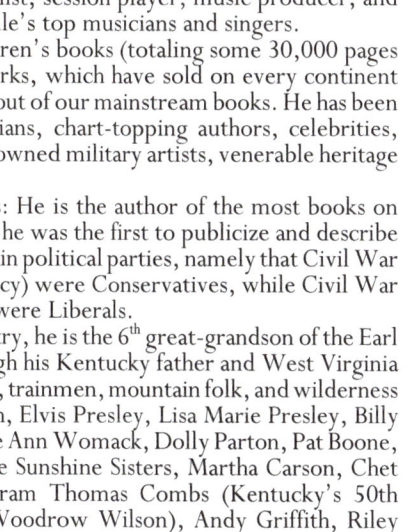

A lifelong litterateur, the Sons of Confederate Veterans member has authored and edited books ranging in topics from ancient and modern history, politics, science, comparative religion, diet and nutrition, spirituality, astronomy, entertainment, military, biography, mysticism, anthropology, cryptozoology, photography, and Bible studies, to natural history, technology, paleography, music, humor, gastronomy, etymology, paleontology, onomastics, mysteries, alternative health and fitness, wildlife, alternate history, comparative mythology, genealogy, Christian history, and the paranormal; books that his readers describe as "game changers," "transformative," and "life altering."

One of America's most popular living historians, nature writers, and Transcendentalists, he is a 17th generation Southerner of Appalachian heritage who descends from dozens of patriotic Revolutionary War soldiers and Confederate soldiers from Kentucky, Tennessee, North Carolina, and Virginia. Also a history, wildlife, and nature preservationist, the well-respected scrivener began life as a child prodigy, later maturing into an archetypal Renaissance Man.

Besides being cofounder and co-CEO of Sea Raven Press, an accomplished writer, author, historian, biographer, lexicographer, encyclopedist, neologist, publisher, editor, poet, polymathic creative, onomastician, etymologist, and Bible authority, the influential prosateur is also a Kentucky Colonel, eagle scout, entrepreneur, businessman, composer, screenwriter, nature, wildlife, and landscape photographer, videographer, and filmmaker, artist, artisan, art director, painter, watercolorist, sculptor, ceramic artist, visual artist, sketch artist, pen and ink artist, graphic artist, graphic designer, book designer, book formatter, editorial designer, book cover designer, publishing designer, Web designer, poster artist, digital artist, cartoonist, content creator, inventor, aquarist, genealogist, ufologist, jewelry designer, jewelry maker, former history museum docent, teacher's assistant, and a former Red Cross certified lifeguard, ranch hand, zookeeper, and wrangler. A contemporary songwriter (of some 3,000 songs in a dozen genres), he is also a pianist, organist, drummer, bass player, rhythm guitarist, rhythm mandolinist, percussionist, electronic musician, synthesist, clavichordist, harpsichordist, classical composer, jingle composer, film composer (currently his musical work has been featured in 11 movies), lyricist, band leader, multi-instrument musician, lead vocalist, backup vocalist, session player, music producer, and recording studio mixing engineer, who has worked and performed with some of Nashville's top musicians and singers.

Currently Seabrook is the multi-genre author and editor of over 100 adult and children's books (totaling some 30,000 pages and 15,000,000 words) that have earned him accolades from around the globe. His works, which have sold on every continent except Antarctica, have introduced hundreds of thousands to vital facts that have been left out of our mainstream books. He has been endorsed internationally by leading experts, museum curators, award-winning historians, chart-topping authors, celebrities, filmmakers, noted scientists, well regarded educators, TV show hosts and producers, renowned military artists, venerable heritage organizations, and distinguished academicians of all races, creeds, and colors.

He currently holds two interesting world records: He is the author of the most books on American military officer Nathan Bedford Forrest, and he was the first to publicize and describe the 19th-Century platform reversal of America's two main political parties, namely that Civil War era Democrats (primarily in the South—the Confederacy) were Conservatives, while Civil War era Republicans (primarily in the North—the Union) were Liberals.

Of northern, western, and central European ancestry, he is the 6th great-grandson of the Earl of Oxford and a descendant of European royalty through his Kentucky father and West Virginia mother. A proud descendant of Appalachian coal miners, trainmen, mountain folk, and wilderness pioneers, his modern day cousins include: Johnny Cash, Elvis Presley, Lisa Marie Presley, Billy Ray and Miley Cyrus, Patty Loveless, Tim McGraw, Lee Ann Womack, Dolly Parton, Pat Boone, Naomi, Wynonna, and Ashley Judd, Ricky Skaggs, the Sunshine Sisters, Martha Carson, Chet Atkins, Patrick J. Buchanan, Cindy Crawford, Bertram Thomas Combs (Kentucky's 50th governor), Edith Bolling (second wife of President Woodrow Wilson), Andy Griffith, Riley Keough, George C. Scott, Robert Duvall, Reese Witherspoon, Lee Marvin, Rebecca Gayheart, and Tom Cruise.

A constitutionalist, avid outdoorsman, wilderness conservationist, and gun rights advocate, Seabrook is the author of the international blockbuster, *Everything You Were Taught About the Civil War is Wrong, Ask a Southerner!* He lives with his wife and family in the magnificent Rocky Mountains, heart of the American West, where you will find him writing, hiking, and filming.

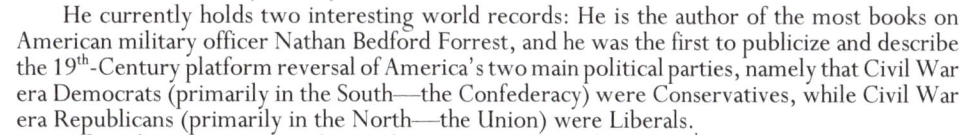

For more information on Mr. Seabrook visit
LochlainnSeabrook.com

Nurture Your Mind, Body, and Spirit!

READ THE BOOKS OF

SEA RAVEN PRESS

Visit our Webstore for a wide selection of wholesome, family-friendly, evidence-based, educational books for all ages. You'll be glad you did!

Artisan-Crafted Books & Merch From the Rocky Mountains

Thank you for supporting our small American family business!

SeaRavenPress.com

Visit our sister sites:
LochlainnSeabrook.com
YouTube.com/user/SeaRavenPress
YouTube.com/@SeabrookFilms
Rumble.com/user/SeaRavenPress
Pond5.com/artist/LochlainnSeabrook

Praise for Author-Historian-Artist

Lochlainn Seabrook

Comments from our readers around the world

✯ "Lochlainn Seabrook is a genius writer!" — STEVEN WARD

✯ "Best author ever." — EMILY

✯ "We get asked a lot what books we use and read. We don't do many modern historians, but we make an exception for some, and Lochlainn Seabrook is one of them. His works are completely well researched from original documents, and heavily footnoted and documented." — SOUTHERN HISTORICAL SOCIETY

✯ "Looking forward to more Lochlainn Seabrook books, my favourite historian!" — ALBERTO IGLESIAS

✯ "Lochlainn Seabrook is one of the finest authors on true history in this century. His books should be on every student's desk." — RONDA SAMMONS RENO

✯ "All of Col. Seabrook's books are great. I have bought most of them and want to end up buying them all." — DAVID VAUGHN

✯ "Lochlainn pulls together such arcane facts with relative ease, compiling these into ordinary prose that strike to the heart with substance, no fluff-speak. I am awestruck! Really. He is an inspiration to me. . . . He is truly a revolutionist. He dares to speak what others whisper; he writes with a boldness and an authoritative knowledge that is second to none." — JAY KRUIZENGA

✯ "Mr. Lochlainn Seabrook is . . . the most well researched and heavily documented author I've ever read. His books are must haves. Everything he writes should be required reading! I assure you, you won't be disappointed. One simply cannot go wrong with his books. Mr. Seabrook is awesome! . . . I have never read any other author as well researched and footnoted as him. I've been in love with Mr. Seabrook for almost 5 years now. His quick wit and logic is enough reason to purchase his books. But the mere fact that he's so extensively researched is icing on the cake. Mr. Seabrook is my favorite, hands down." — LANI BURNETTE RINKEL

✯ "My favorite book is the Bible. Lochlainn Seabrook wrote my second favorite book." — RICHARD FINGER

✯ "I have a new favorite author and his name is Lochlainn Seabrook." — J. EWING

✯ "Lochlainn Seabrook is an incredible writer and I love all of his books on the South. . . . His writing is brilliant. . . . I look forward to reading more of his masterpieces. Thank you." — JOEY

✯ "It's hard to choose just one of Lochlainn's books!" — ROSANNE STEELE

✯ "Mr. Seabrook, thank you ever so much for blessing us with your most enlightening works." — LAURENCE DRURY

✯ "I recommend anything written by Lochlainn Seabrook." — HOTRODMOB

✯ "Awesome books . . . by a great writer of truth, Lochlainn. Thank you so much. Keep up the great work you do." — WILDBUNCH19INF

✯ "I love Lochlainn Seabrook's style and approach. It's not the 'norm.' What a miracle his books are. . . . He is a literal life changing author! Amazing books!" — KEITH PARISH

✯ "I adore Mr. Seabrook's style and I love his books. I love an author that does proper research, and still finds a way to engage the reader. Mr. Seabrook does an admirable job of both." — DONALD CAUL

✯ "Lochlainn Seabrook's books are much more well researched and authoritative than those eminently celebrated as being the authorities on the subjects he writes on. You can always trust to find the truth in his writings. . . . He does not rewrite history, but instead shows it as it is." — GARY STIER

✯ "I love all of Colonel Seabrook's books. They are informative and enlightening, and his warm Southern hospitality writing style makes you feel right at home." — KEITH CRAVEN

✯ "Lochlainn Seabrook's work is an absolute treasure of scholarship and historic scope." — MARK WAYNE CUNNINGHAM

✯ "Mr. Seabrook's command of . . . history is breathtaking. . . . He deserves great renown—check out his books!" — MARGARET SIMMONS

✯ "I love Seabrook's writings. LOVE!!! . . . So grateful to know the truth! Keep writing Lochlainn!!!" — REBECCA DALRYMPLE

✯ "Lochlainn Seabrook . . . [has] probably [written] the best book on mental science in existence by a living author. Along with Thomas Troward, Emmet Fox, and Jack Addington, Mr. Seabrook is one of the top four mental science authors of all time, since biblical times." - IAN BARTON STEWART

✯ "Glad I discovered Mr. Seabrook! . . . He writes eye opening books! Unbelievable the facts he unearths - and he backs it all up with truth, notes, footnotes, and bibliography! . . . He always amazes me! His books always see the whole picture. His timelines and bibliographies are incredible. He always provides carefully reasoned arguments! He's the best. To me I think he's better than the late great Shelby Foote! America needs more like Lochlainn Seabrook. I can't wait to own all of his books on the war someday. Everyone who wants the Truth, who seeks the Truth and wants the full story, should read his books." — JOHN BULL BADER

✯ "Amazing books for people who actually want to know the truth. Seabrook's skill in writing and researching has no equal since the great Shelby Foote. If I could rate his books more than 5 stars I would." — CANDICE

✯ "I love all of Colonel Seabrook's books!" — DEBBIE SIDLE

✯ "Lochlainn Seabrook is well educated and versed in what he writes and I'm impressed with the delivery." — THOMAS L. WHITE

✯ "Lochlainn Seabrook is the author of great works of scholarship." — JOHN B.

✯ "Thank you Lochlainn Seabrook for your wonderful books! You are the real deal! You are an amazing author and I love your books!!" — SOPHIA MEOW CELLIST

✯ "I really enjoy Mr. Seabrook's books! His knowledge is beyond belief!" — SANDRA FISH

✯ "Love Lochlainn Seabrook. Awesome!!" — ROBIN HENDERSON ARISTIDES

✯ "Kudos to Lochlainn Seabrook who is a very good and informative professional truthful historian. We need more like him!" — AMY VACHON

If you enjoyed this book you will be interested in Colonel Seabrook's complete Forrest book collection:

- A Rebel Born: A Defense of Nathan Bedford Forrest (winner of the Jefferson Davis Historical Gold Medal).
- A Rebel Born: The Screenplay.
- Forrest! 99 Reasons to Love Nathan Bedford Forrest.
- Give 'Em Hell Boys: The Complete Military Correspondence of Nathan Bedford Forrest.
- I Rode with Forrest: Confederate Soldiers Who Served With the World's Greatest Cavalry Leader.
- Nathan Bedford Forrest and African-Americans: Yankee Myth, Confederate Fact.
- Nathan Bedford Forrest and the Battle of Fort Pillow: Yankee Myth, Confederate Fact.
- Nathan Bedford Forrest and the Ku Klux Klan: Yankee Myth, Confederate Fact.
- Nathan Bedford Forrest: Southern Hero, American Patriot.
- Saddle, Sword and Gun: A Biography of Nathan Bedford Forrest For Teens.
- The God of War: Nathan Bedford Forrest As He Was Seen By His Contemporaries.
- The Illustrated Nathan Bedford Forrest: An American Patriot's Life in Pictures.
- The Quotable Nathan Bedford Forrest: Selections From the Writings and Speeches of the Confederacy's Most Brilliant Cavalryman.

Available from Sea Raven Press and wherever fine books are sold.

Forrest age 35. Copyright © L.S.

Forrest age 51. Copyright © L.S.

PLEASE VISIT OUR WEBSTORE FOR A COMPLETE LIST OF COLONEL SEABROOK'S BOOKS & ARTWORK, INCLUDING HIS FINE ART PHOTO PRINTS, WALL POSTERS, BUMPER STICKERS, POSTCARDS, CALENDARS, & BOOKMARKS.

SeaRavenPress.com

www.ingramcontent.com/pod-product-compliance
Lightning Source LLC
Chambersburg PA
CBHW060936170426
43194CB00026B/2972